SOME SHORTISH HOMILIES
for Advent and Christmas

GLORIFYING
THE LORD
BY YOUR LIFE

James O'Kane

*In grateful remembrance of my parents
who first acquainted me with
the drama of the Mass*

**James O'Kane
Second Officer, Merchant Navy
Born Cushendall 1915
Died Manaus 1963**

**Rose O'Kane
née Connolly
Born Latton 1914
Died Whiteabbey 1989**

Requiescant in pace

Acknowledgment

Use has been made throughout of the English version of Volume I of the Roman Lectionary approved for use in Ireland in 1981.

The Homilist

Father James O'Kane was born in Belfast where he received his earliest education from Dominican Sisters and at Christian Brothers' schools. After seminary formation in Belfast and Rome he undertook postgraduate studies at Louvain and was ordained in 1976. From 1979 he taught spiritual and moral theology at Maynooth. Since 1995 he has served in Newtownards & Comber, Ballintoy & Ballinlea, Culfeightrin, Kilcoo and Cushendun & Torr.

ADVENT

First Sunday of Advent

A.

The night is almost over, it will be daylight soon - let us give up all the things we prefer to do under the cover of the dark.

The season of Advent, brothers and sisters in Christ, is a time of preparation for our Christmas celebration of the birth of Jesus - the birth of Jesus in Bethlehem, the birth of Jesus in human history, the birth of Jesus in the hearts of all who accept him as their Lord and Saviour. Christmas has been stolen from us and commercialised beyond all recognition. We get caught up in all that ourselves and so it is not easy for us to stop and live these Advent days in the simple, quiet way that prepares the birth of God in the human heart.

In Advent we learn to wait. We are, of course, always waiting for something. What we are waiting for makes us the sort of people we are. Advent challenges us to say what it is that we are really waiting for, what it is that we really expect of life, what we hope will ultimately become of us. Advent reminds us that we are waiting for God.

There is hope in such waiting. We all have particular hopes of our own, of course. Our hopes keep us alive. Where there's hope there's life. To live at all is to hope that things will change for the better. We have hopes for ourselves, for our families, for our country, for our world. And underlying all our hopes we recognise a thirst for love and friend-ship, a thirst for justice and truth, a thirst that can never be content with things as they are. And we recognise too the limits of our human hopes: our failures and disappointments, the inevitability of disease, disability and death.

Christians are Advent people drawing life and strength from a hope that beckons to us from outside and beyond this present world. When we say that Jesus himself is our hope we do not camouflage, much less escape, the real difficulties of human life. Our hope in Jesus strengthens our commitment to reality. Our hope in Jesus invites us to organise all our hopes around him. His wisdom shows us what is really important and invites us to cast aside all that is trivial. Because we hope in Jesus we are committed to working to bring about the change we hope for, in our lives and in our world. We work, no longer on our own, hindered by human weakness, but carried forward by the kindness of God given to us in his Son at Christmas.

Perhaps just now our hearts are too cluttered for Jesus to find a home there. If we could use these Advent days to unclutter our hearts in welcome we might well find Jesus waiting for us this year in Christmas.

The night is almost over, it will be daylight soon - let us give up all the things we prefer to do under the cover of the dark.

Isaiah 2:1-5 / Romans 13:11-14 / Matthew 24:3

3

B.

May God our Father and the Lord Jesus Christ send you grace and peace.

Advent, brothers and sisters in Christ, like so many opportunities that come our way in life, is what we make of it. That is why we might want to pause today and decide for ourselves what we might like to make of our Advent this year.

Advent is an invitation to start again at the beginning. To start again at the beginning - in the sense of following more consciously the Church's calendar that will lead us through Christmas to Easter and beyond to Pentecost. To start again at the be-ginning - in the sense of seizing hold of the remnants of our Christian faith and committing ourselves afresh to its practical outworking in our daily lives. The resolve, in the words of today's Collect, to run forth to meet God's Christ with righteous deeds at his coming, so that, gathered at his right hand, we may be worthy to possess the heavenly kingdom.

For all of us Advent can be a time of grace, an opportunity to start again, to take a different approach, to be open to the presence of God in our lives in a new and hope-filled way. We could adopt an Advent stance. We could create Advent moments of stillness in our sometimes hectic lives as yet another year hurtles towards its end. For all of us, whatever our past, whatever our present, the promise of Advent is that Christmas could this time round be a rich and fresh experience of peace and joy, if only we were courageous enough to use these days and weeks to open our minds and hearts in readiness and in faith.

Advent renews the call of Jesus for us to stay awake and keep vigil, in sobriety and in hope, in expectation and in prayer. Be on your guard, he urges us, stay awake because you do not know when the master is coming. If he comes unexpectedly, he must not find you asleep. Stay awake.

Advent is about staying awake and waiting attentively for Jesus. Waiting for Jesus is what gives us our identity as Christians. Are we in fact waiting for Jesus, or for something else? It's not yet too late to start asking ourselves honestly what it is that we are really waiting for, what it is that we genuinely expect of life, what we hope will ultimately become of us. What we are in fact waiting for determines the sort of people that we are. Tell me what you are waiting for and you'll have said more about yourself than maybe you meant to say.

Humanity has been forever waiting for God, perhaps without knowing it. We have been waiting for Jesus, perhaps much too tentatively. Advent is an invitation to start again at the very beginning.

May God our Father and the Lord Jesus Christ send you grace and peace.

Isaiah   63:16-17;   64:1.3-8   /   First Corinthians 1:3-9 / Mark 13:33-37

C.

We urge you and appeal to you in the Lord Jesus to make more and more progress in the kind of life you are meant to live: the life that God wants.

Advent, brothers and sisters in Christ, is an invitation to take things a stage further. An invitation to allow ourselves at last to be fully embraced by the mercy of God.

The Advent call is the call of Jesus to every Christian generation. We are to stay awake and keep vigil, in sobriety and in hope, in expectation and in prayer. We are to make more and more progress in the kind of life we are meant to live: the life that God wants. What is this life that God wants?

Those of us who are older are coming out of a time when religious people got so caught up in the details that they lost sight of the big picture. Perhaps we need to apologise to our young people for that, if ever again we could get their attention. We are always forgetting the essential. What I want, God reminds us in three words that should echo constantly in the heart of every disciple, what I want is mercy, not sacrifice. Mercy, not sacrifice. What God wants is mercy and more and more progress in the kind of life we are meant to live.

Perhaps too many of us have not yet in our own lives experienced the mercy of God. We think to get away with a gruesome sacrifice of one kind or another when what God our Father wants is that we should be merciful to one another as he has been merciful to us. Let us have the courage then to welcome this Advent grace. When we fail in our Advent vigilance our hearts are quickly coarsened by a very understandable animal quest for comfort and pleasure which leaves us coldly indifferent to our Father in heaven and his children, our brothers and sisters, suffering on our doorsteps and around the world.

What God wants from us is mercy - and more and more of it.

First Sunday of Advent

Jeremiah 33:14-16 / First Thessalonians 3:13-4:2 / Luke 21:25-28.34-36

The Immaculate Conception of the Blessed Virgin Mary (8th December)

Behold the handmaid of the Lord, she said. Be it done unto me according to thy word.

Mary leads the way, brothers and sisters in Christ, in humility and in obedience. But we seem more inclined to admire than to follow. Whatever we may be called to ourselves, it is unlikely to involve, for us any more than it did for her, a comfortable conformity to convention and tradition. Doing the will of God, for us as for Mary, will involve something new, something startling and unsettling. And from where we stand it is not at all clear that whatever we might receive as our reward for doing the will of God would really be worth the sacrifice of self that humility and obedience would require of us here and now.

From where we stand.... Here and now.... If we leave the simplicity and transparency of today's Gospel and turn back to that extract from the book of Genesis we find ourselves perhaps in more familiar territory. There we see what becomes of human beings when they turn away from God in the pursuit of self. There we see what becomes of us when we do not seek the will of God but only the mirage that the fascination of evil persuades us is our own divinity.

Where are you? - the Lord God called to the man. Where are you? God comes looking for us to remind us that he loves us and that we belong with him. But we in our guilt and shame cannot face him. I heard the sound of you in the garden. I was afraid because I was naked and so I hid. But how else are we to appear before God if not in all the nakedness of our need?

He knows our fear and offers us the grace of confession and forgiveness. He already knows the truth about us and he offers to help us to face that truth. Who told you that you were naked? Have you been eating of the tree I forbade you to eat? But how often have we not had this very experience. We are too afraid to own our guilt and grace passes us by. Instead of seizing the opportunity of confession we blame someone else. It was the woman you put with me. She gave me the fruit, and I ate it. The serpent tempted me and I ate. In this Adam and Eve are indeed our first parents, the father and mother of us all. In a perverse way the blame is thrown back at God himself: you made the world this way, you made me this way - it's all your fault. And so we are locked in an undying struggle with the serpent. Again and again just when we think we have crushed his head he strikes our heel, in a vicious circle until the end of time. Or until we are set free. For when we are tired of having everything our own way we find that God is still there, waiting for us, asking where we are and hinting what it might be best for us to do next.

Behold the handmaid of the Lord, she said. Be it done unto me according to thy word. Mary leads the way, in humility and in obedience. We would do well to follow her.

O Mary, conceived without sin, pray for us who have recourse to thee.

Genesis 3:9-15. 20 / Ephesians 1:3-6. 11-12 / Luke 1:26-38

Second Sunday of Advent

A.

Prepare a way for the Lord. Make his paths straight.

It may no longer be possible, brothers and sisters in Christ, to retrieve any public sense of Advent as a time of spiritual preparation for the feast of Christmas. There was a time, though, that those of us who are older remember, when these holy Advent days were lived in a frugal simplicity that allowed the joy of Christmas to burst upon the disciples of Jesus on Christmas Eve launching them on the twelve days of celebration that ended with Epiphany on 6th January. Nowadays "Christmas" starts to build up several weeks before 25th December and then quickly peters out in the bleakness of the last days of the old year, the leftovers and the sales. It is the world we live in and who would say that we should not be part of it? And yet....

And yet a voice cries in the wilderness: Prepare a way for the Lord. Make straight his paths. Perhaps "Christmas" is not the best time of the year to try to talk to people about Christ. They are too busy. Some of them too busy even to enjoy themselves. And yet...

And yet, is it not at the very heart of the world's festive fever at "Christmas" that so many people catch a glimpse of their own inner emptiness and despair? Is it not the time of the year when the absence of God from people's lives is most glaringly obvious?

A voice cries in the wilderness: Prepare a way for the Lord. Make straight his paths. Any public sense of Advent may have been lost, and with our collusion. But we are still free, as individuals and as families, to adopt an Advent stance, to contrive some gesture or symbol to remind us that the deeper meaning of our lives is in our waiting for God.

There is nothing more glorious than the birth of God in the human soul. Our lives are Advent lives. We are preparing a way for the Lord. Our hearts open in welcome as we repent. The things that hinder us from receiving him with joy fall away as our sins are forgiven. It is in the wilderness of our own personal world that the word of God comes to us. Everything that was written long ago in the scriptures, St Paul reminds us, was meant to teach us something about hope, about how people who did not give up were helped by God.

If we are truly repentant, it is high time we started producing the appropriate fruit. Many of us are so blinded by the self-satisfaction of not finding any of the really big sins on our conscience that we miss the biggest sin of all – our failure to do anything much for Jesus. Perhaps we could make a list of all the many things we fail to do and bring it with us to our next confession.

Isaiah 11:1-10 / Romans 15:4-9 / Matthew 3:1-12

B.

The beginning of the Good News about Jesus Christ, the Son of God.

Advent, brothers and sisters in Christ, is an invitation to start again at the beginning. The dramatic figure of John the Baptist heralded, in his day, just such a new beginning. He appeared in the wilderness of Judaea proclaiming a baptism of repentance for the forgiveness of sins. All kinds of people made their way to him and as they were baptised by him in the river Jordan they confessed their sins.

We are Christians. Jesus himself has baptised us with the Holy Spirit of God making us his living presence in the world of today. What possible interest has John the Baptist for us? Why does the Church insist on reminding us of him Advent after Advent? It could just be that we still need to be summoned back, right back to the beginning, and told to start again. For this is the beginning of the good news about Jesus Christ, the Son of God. The voice crying in the wilderness: Prepare a way for the Lord. John the Baptist was that voice then. We are called to be that voice today. For we are called to cry out to others what we have first heard in our own hearts. The wilderness is the same for us all, however different the decorations, however generous the consolations.

The most remarkable effect of John the Baptist was that those who came to him confessed their sins. It is still an indispensable first step. Our sins cannot be forgiven until they have first been confessed. For confession is a moment of self-knowledge, facilitated by the listening ear of another and it brings a forgiveness that heals. Anything else is a comfortless self-deception that leaves us in our pain.

Yes, Jesus came to take away the sins of the world. But he is powerless to take away our sins until we are ready to let go. Yes, Jesus came to call sinners. But we are slow to accept that that means us. For it is only in the moment of confession that we know our sin. Yes, Jesus came to heal the contrite. But we cannot be contrite until the time is right. Our hope of healing first whispers to us in the voice crying in our wilderness: Prepare a way for the Lord, make his paths straight. Such indeed is the beginning of the good news of Jesus for us.

Perhaps our hearts are today like that famous inn at Bethlehem, too full to accommodate his birth within us. Unburdening ourselves of our sins would be a first step in making our hearts more like the Christmas stable, an unlikely place, but empty and waiting, and ready for the birth of God.

Isaiah 40:1-5. 9-11 / Second Peter 3:8-14 / Mark 1:1-8

C.

A voice cries in the wilderness.

Sometimes the silence of God weighs heavily upon us, brothers and sisters in Christ, and the cold and darkness of our hearts is almost more than we can bear. We are ready for a John the Baptist, someone to stand up and denounce the hypocrisy and injustice we see around us, someone to call corruption by its name, demand radical changes in the Church and in society, and dramatically point the way forward.

And yet such strident preaching, not to mention all the crusades and inquisitions to which it gives rise, has never proved very effective as a stratagem against evil. And this for the simple reason that direct assaults on the symptoms of human sinfulness, terrorise or entertain us though they may, depending on our mood, do nothing to heal the sickness itself. Our problem is not with what we do but with what we are. Our occasional sins would be of less account but for the fact that they reveal us for the sinners that we permanently are at our core. Tinkering with our sins is not even a short term solution, particularly if it camouflages the fact that we are sinners through and through.

Most of us live with too little awareness of how consistent we actually are. Our lives at best can be given a certain charm. At worst they are all shallowness and triviality. They are made up of this and that. We do some good here and there. We intersperse our good deeds with much silliness. Every so often we make a completely fresh start. We drift through life and never have the experience of putting it all together. We never have an overall view of ourselves as consistently sinful. We do not really know who we are.

The one thing necessary - and the most difficult thing - is to detach our attention from everything outside ourselves and accept the terrible moment of loneliness without which it will never be possible to know ourselves as we are. To learn the truth about our lives there must be silence in our hearts. We begin to create that silence by shutting out what other people think of us, the unsought advice they press upon us, their praise that flatters us, their blame that intimidates us.

When we do this, and let us not pretend that it is easy, when we create this silence within us, we begin to hear a voice crying in our own personal wilderness: Prepare a way for the Lord. It is a voice that is strangely familiar, the voice of our own truest self that we have perhaps never really heard before.

Baruch 5:1-9 / Philippians 1:3-6. 8-11 / Luke 3:1-6

Third Sunday of Advent

A.

Those the Lord has ransomed shall return. They will come to Zion shouting for joy, everlasting joy on their faces; joy and gladness will go with them and sorrow and lament be ended.

Gaudete Sunday, brothers and sisters in Christ, as the third Sunday of Advent is traditionally known from the first word of the entrance antiphon, invites us to celebrate our joy as Christians, our joy at being alive, our joy at being saved in Jesus. Gaudete in Domino semper. Rejoice in the Lord always; again I say, rejoice. Indeed, the Lord is near.

Our joy in Jesus is no foolish elation. It is a sober joy, a patient joy, an Advent joy as we watch for the day, hoping that the salvation promised us will be ours when the Lord comes again in his glory. On the one hand an immense joy because Jesus has come to be our Saviour. And on the other hand a call to patient, hope-filled perseverance as we wait for Jesus to come again. Joy - because the seed of God's kingdom has been sown among us. Patience - because the kingdom has not yet come in all its fullness. If we have ceased to witness to the joy that has been potentially the fruit of the Holy Spirit in our hearts since our Baptism, if we have become so little bothered about perseverance that we have quite forgotten that Jesus is to return, then Advent summons us back to our vocation as Christians, a vocation of joyful perseverance until he comes again.

Being made to wait, of course, nourishes doubt. John the Baptist has been nothing if not consistent and absolutely clear but in prison and facing death he begins to wonder about Jesus. Are you the one who is to come, he wants to know, or have we got to wait for someone else? Jesus does not oblige with a yes or no answer. He leaves John in his doubt. He leaves him to make up his own mind and we really do not know his final mind about Jesus and his mission.

John has been the messenger sent ahead to prepare the way. Jesus cannot praise him highly enough: of all the children born of women, a greater than John the Baptist has never been seen. But Jesus himself marks a new departure. He sets out in a direction John might not easily have imagined so that the least in the kingdom of heaven is greater than John. Certainly John preached a return to an ancient and beneficial integrity but the kingdom of Jesus is much more than that. Beyond all personal moral achievement it is a kingdom of grace where all is sheer gift. The blind see again, the lame walk, lepers are cleansed, the deaf hear, the dead are raised to life and, above all, the Good News is proclaimed to the poor.

This is the promise that sustains our Advent joy. This is the hope that enlivens our patient perseverance. Our every Christmas strengthens our faith in Jesus. Our every Christmas draws us further into his kingdom where joy and gladness will be forever our companions and sorrow and lament be ended once and for all.

Glorifying the Lord by Your Life

Isaiah 35:1-6. 10 / James 5:7-10 / Matthew 11:2-11

B.

Be happy at all times.
Pray constantly. And for all things
give thanks to God.

Certain forms of Christianity are remarkable, brothers and sisters in Christ, for their grim faces and dreary lives. As Saint Paul today reminds us, God expects Christians to be happy at all times, to pray constantly and to give thanks to him for all things. It is somehow inappropriate for the disciples of Jesus to look sad and have gloomy faces. Gaudete in Domino semper. Rejoice in the Lord always; again I say rejoice! Indeed, the Lord is near.

We all know, of course, that it is not at all easy to rejoice. It is not always easy even to be cheerful. So perhaps we might pause today to consider the obstacles to joy in our lives and how they might be overcome. Above all there is the suffering we bring upon ourselves by our attitude, the way we react to our own personal circumstances. Our refusal to come to terms with the reality of our personal

27

situation, our failure to accept ourselves as we really are only serves to aggravate our frustration and exasperation. Even the minor irritations of everyday life can become a serious obstacle to joy. We are in so many ways too demanding. We moan and complain and grumble and joy passes us by. We take ourselves too seriously. We expect too much of everyone and every-thing: - the perfect recipe for a permanent state of annoyance, anger, rage.

The Lord is near: Rejoice! The message of all true religion is that there is a way out of this paralysing self-pity. True believers are sent as messengers of joy to prepare a way for the Lord in a world that has turned in on itself and away from God. But we cannot usefully rush out into the world with our message of joy before we have attended to our own inner wilderness. It is in that process of conversion and repentance that Jesus is born in our hearts and begins to shine through our lives as the light of our world. In that light self-pity gives way before self-acceptance. Self-absorption is dissolved in a genuine concern for others. God's joy is waiting to surprise us in every moment - in the people around us, in our daily tasks of love and service, in our prayer and in the healing silence of our hearts. We become Advent people waiting in hope and patience for our God.

At the end God will no doubt disappoint those who expect him to be sorry for them. He will want to know instead that we have enjoyed the life he gave us, for it is the only life we are ever going to have and really we need never have been at all. In the meantime this Advent season inviting us to a greater simplicity of life and prayerful preparation for the coming feast is a stratagem devised by the Church to help us become truly Christmas people, for our own sake and for the salvation of our world.

Isaiah 61:1-2. 10-11 / First Thessalonians 5:16-24 / John 1:6-8. 19-28

C.

Rejoice in the Lord always; again I say rejoice! The Lord is near.

Joy, brothers and sisters in Christ, is one of the fruits of the Holy Spirit of God, together with love and peace. Christian joy possesses a solidity that distinguishes it unmistakeably from the false hilarity of intoxication and elation. It is a divine gift. It cannot be earned or achieved. It cannot be faked. Advent invites us back to active preparation for receiving it. We are invited to open our minds, our hearts, our lives in readiness.

But Christian joy, just like any other gift, can be refused altogether, or once accepted then neglected and even destroyed. Advent creates a sense of expectancy within the inevitable turmoil of our disappointment and despair. The Lord is near: Rejoice! There must surely be a way out of our prison, if only we could find it. The promise of Advent is that something might happen this time round. Something new, something real, in the world, in the Church, in us, in our lives, in our families. Some change for the better could actually happen, and soon. Change for the better is just waiting to happen for us, a real possibility lurking in every moment.

Take the people in today's Gospel for instance. They are quite ordinary people, people not too different from ourselves really, despite the centuries that separate us. Suddenly and unexpectedly confronted by the dramatic figure of John the Baptist they find themselves intimately challenged about who they are and the way they live. We sense the urgency of their question. What must we do then, they want to know. Yes, sometimes, in our distraction, in the turmoil of our lives, we need someone gifted with distance and common sense to point out the obvious to us. That it is always better to share no matter how little we think we have. That we are never to exploit one another even when we have the opportunity to get away with it. That we are to do our work, in simplicity and thankfulness, without degrading others or damaging ourselves. Such are the keys to the floodgates of joy.

John the Baptist is ready with a personal word for everyone who asks. But they do have to ask first. We all know from bitter experience how useless it is to point out the obvious without waiting to be asked. And perhaps from that experience we learn our own need to be open to some word about the all too obvious that we have not yet felt able to hear.

The promise of Advent to each and every one of us is that, whoever we are, wherever we are at in our lives, there can be at last a beginning of joy. In our waiting for God we all too easily forget that God is waiting for us. He is nearer to us than we are to ourselves.

Christmas can be so much more than just another chance for another fresh start. For there is this talk too of a Baptism with the Holy Spirit - and the holy fire of real living. In Jesus God comes to share in our humanity so that we might dare to begin to lay hold of his divinity.

Third Sunday of Advent

Zephaniah 3:14-16 / Philippians 4:4-7 / Luke 3:10-18

Fourth Sunday of Advent

A.

This is how Jesus Christ came to be born.

Today's gospel, brothers and sisters in Christ, invites us to see the Christmas story through the eyes of Joseph. His drama is told soberly and concisely: This is how Jesus Christ came to be born. His mother Mary was betrothed to Joseph – but before they came to live together she was found to be with child through the Holy Spirit. We can well imagine that Joseph's first reaction to this shock was the absurd one that we are all familiar with. Why should this happen to me? He is no doubt a decent young man and he decides that it would be best to break off the relationship quietly, put the incident behind him and get on with his life.

Why should this happen to me? But why not? Is it not absurd to assume that we have a right to get on with our lives in our own wilful way and at the same time claim to believe in a

God of surprises? A right to get on with our lives – what lives? Are we not pathetic caricatures of ourselves when we doggedly pursue our own agenda to the end of our days while all the time paying lip-service to the wisdom of a God who has his own inexorable plan for each one of us. We stamp our feet and scream, children who have never grown up, deaf to the message of divine wisdom that maturity and freedom are nothing other than a gracious cooperation with the inevitable.

For this miracle to happen we need, like Joseph, our own angel and our own dream. Other peoples' visions are second-hand and no use to us at all. Joseph had already made up his mind what to do when the angel of the Lord appeared to him in a dream and said: Joseph, son of David, do not be afraid to take Mary home as your wife, because she has conceived what is in her by the Holy Spirit. She will give birth to a son and you must name him Jesus, because he is the one who is to save his people from their sins. When Joseph woke up he did what the angel of the Lord had told him to do. Instead of getting on with his own life he provided a home and respectability for Mary and her child. This was the unexpected meaning of his life, his vocation. We never hear of him again but we know that he was happy for the Church has always honoured him as a saint.

Happiness and holiness are not the outcome of the dogged pursuit of our own agenda. They are what happen to us when we are doing something else altogether. This is the miracle Jesus offers us. It is all too often our own personal tragedy that we are not ready for this salvation. We are so far from thinking that we need to be saved at all that we miss our moments of grace. And most of all we need to be saved from ourselves. Joseph had made up his mind to do the right and decent thing. The angel of the Lord appeared to him in a dream and told him to do something dramatically different.

Let us allow Jesus to save us. Let us allow him to do what he came to do, to work his miracle, to draw us into the mystery of his cross and resurrection where we will receive our freedom in gracious cooperation with the inevitable. Let us look for a quiet moment in these closing days of Advent to attend to the voice of our angel and begin to obey our dream. For this is still how Jesus Christ comes to be born today.

Isaiah 7:10-14 / Romans 1:1-7 / Matthew 1:18-24

B.

Mary, do not be afraid. You have won God's favour.

Do not be afraid. These are the first words God speaks to us, brothers and sisters in Christ, every time he threatens to touch our lives.

Christmas reminds us of a time of innocence, a time before fear came, a time that did not last. Somehow, all too soon, we left innocence behind and surrendered to a sinful world. Somehow we all grow up crooked and away from God. As we look for a way back to where we belong Mary is given to us as the template of our own discipleship. By her humility and her obedience she is the pattern and model of our return to God.

Luke's account of the annunciation is familiar to us from our prayer. Hail Mary, full of grace, the Lord is with thee. It is Gabriel's greeting. The angel of the Lord declared unto Mary. The Angelus sums up and recalls the event. Mary was deeply disturbed by the angel's words. She had not anticipated this divine intrusion and could not imagine where it might lead. Our own situation is not different when we wonder why we are where we are and cannot grasp what it is that God is calling us to nor understand the purpose behind our joys and sorrows. Gabriel reassured her. Mary, do not be afraid. You have won God's favour. Listen! You are to conceive and bear a son.

And she conceived of the Holy Spirit. It is interesting to speculate what would have happened if Mary had refused this highly unusual invitation. Indeed it is quite possible that Mary was not the first woman to be asked to mother our Saviour. But Mary's humble obedience is the key to God's success. Behold the handmaid of the Lord. Be it done unto me according to thy word. Through Mary's generosity the Word became flesh and dwelt amongst us - full of grace and truth and we have beheld his glory, glory as of the only Son from the Father. And from his fullness we have all received, grace upon grace.

This is the true story of Christmas and we are all invited to be part of it. Of course we are afraid - the sinner's life is riddled with anxiety - but we are called beyond all that into freedom, the glorious liberty of the children of God. When we imitate Mary's humility and obedience by being open to God's will for us in our everyday lives the Spirit brings Jesus to birth in our hearts, the glory of God refreshes our world, others too are graced. And the innocence of Christmas returns.

Second Samuel 7:1-5. 8-12. 14. 16 / Romans 16:25-27 / Luke 1:26-38

C.

Yes, blessed is she who believed that the promise made her by the Lord would be fulfilled.

At the heart of Christmas, brothers and sisters in Christ, there is a woman who holds a unique place in the great human story of which we are all of us invited to be part. Of all women Mary is the most blessed because she accepted God's invitation to be the mother of his Son, Our Lord and Saviour Jesus Christ. Behold the handmaid of the Lord, she said, be it done unto me according to thy word. She is the mother too of all who follow her example: her example of humility, her example of obedience.

No indeed, Mary's virtues are not popular in the world around us. They seem the very enemies of the success and satisfaction the world preaches. But the disciples of Jesus know that to be children of Mary by following her example is to renew the miracle of Christmas in their own time and place.

The miracle of Christmas that somehow eludes us as we send our cards and deliver our presents and make our annual visits hovers tantalizingly in Mary's visit to her cousin Elizabeth. The simple kindness of one woman to another. An ordinary joy. Sharing and being together. Perhaps our own lives, like our Christmases, have become too complicated for such simple kindnesses and such ordinary joys. Why should I be honoured with a visit from the mother of my Lord? - Elizabeth wonders. Has all wonder died? What happens when we meet one another?

Do we really meet at all in the hectic rush of our daily round and the frenzy of our pagan Christmas? Does it ever occur to us to stop and marvel at our own mystery and the mystery of those who people our lives? Why should I be honoured with a visit from this sister, this brother of my Lord?

Has all freshness gone from such encounters? Neglected friendships, unknown neighbours, husbands and wives who take each other too much for granted, parents and children who have become strangers to one another. Mary's example teaches us to be humble and reverent towards one another, to seek to serve rather than to use and abuse, to expect miracles instead of despairing of those around us.

Elizabeth, filled with the Holy Spirit, rightly identifies the source of Mary's happiness and the kindness and joy that flow from it: Blessed is she who believed that the promise made her by the Lord would be fulfilled. Christmas is a reminder of God's promise to each one of us and an invitation to believe with all our hearts that that promise will be fulfilled. When we follow Mary's example, when we make our own those words the Letter to the Hebrews gives to Jesus in the moment of his incarnation: God, here I am! I am coming to obey your will - then we too are gifted with the

Holy Spirit and God lives again in us and in our world.

Micah 5:1-4 / Hebrews 10:5-10 / Luke 1:39-44

CHRISTMAS

The Nativity of the Lord

I.

A Saviour has been born to you. He is Christ the Lord. And here is a sign for you: you will find a baby wrapped in swaddling clothes and lying in a manger.

Nostalgia and sentimentality, brothers and sisters in Christ, help to fill our churches at Christmas. Our restless hearts urge us fleetingly to look in on God to see if he is still there. God, as we might expect, is always at home - it we who have gone walkabout. Nostalgia and sentimentality lay hold of us at Christmas and entice us back to the security and comfort of home. It is rarely a particularly intense experience but it can be an opportunity for grace to strike, a starting point for a genuine con-version and a real personal awakening to our radical need for God.

We all have our own reasons, then, for being here. And we all bring with us the burdens of our lives, the burdens we have accumulated over the years, the burdens we have become to ourselves. Perhaps we could think of leaving all these burdens, or at least some of them, or maybe even just one of them, behind us at the crib this Christmas. For these burdens of ours are truly the most precious gifts we could offer Jesus on his birthday. Nothing could please him more than to see us free and unburdened, alive at last, at Christmas. That is, after all, why he came into our world. That is what he lived for. That is what he died for on the cross.

Our churches, it is true, are never quite as crowded on Good Friday. Nostalgia and sentimentality can get us started again if we have stalled but they will not, on their own, bring us anywhere near the Easter of personal resurrection, much less the Pentecost of shared responsibility for the presence of God's Holy Spirit in our lives and in our world.

The shadow of the cross lies over the crib and we are blind not to see it for it is the sign of our hope, our only real hope, the promise of our own final victory over suffering and death. The Christmas story is a cluster of signs pointing us towards this one great sign of Christian hope, a baby wrapped in swaddling clothes and lying in a manger, a family for whom there was no room at the inn, shepherds watching their flocks in the night, angels giving glory to God and offering peace to all men and women of good will.

Save us. Saviour of the world, for by your cross and resurrection you have set us free. You are our peace and our joy forever.

II.

But the angel said, "Do not be afraid. Listen, I bring you news of great joy, a joy to be shared by the whole people."

Christmas, brothers and sisters in Christ, every year creates a sense of expectancy. Something might really happen, something new, some change for the better. There is a hint of a new dawn, the seeds of a new hope, the chance of a new beginning. Our lives, distorted as they so often are by all kinds of fears and anxieties, can be caught up in this Christmas enthusiasm and transformed beyond our wildest imaginings.

The winter festival that was always a moment of joy celebrated the birth of a new sun, the sure promise of a new spring, another summer. Our far off ancestors, startled by the shortening days of winter, thought the sun was dying and were afraid. As the days began to lengthen they were reassured. Fear turned to joy and celebration. At some deep, primitive level the same rhythm of fear and joy still echoes at the core of our being. For like most living things we wither in the dark. We need the light for our flourishing and our fulfilment.

The Christian vision of our human destiny promises a different kind of light in a more personal darkness. At a certain point in our lives we become aware of our dying. We feel lost and irrelevant in the immensity of the universe. We search for meaning. We curse the entanglements that have blinded us and distracted us from the true meaning of our lives, entanglements that we have freely chosen and yet somehow not chosen at all. We are afraid in our darkness. We surrender to despair.

All too often such indeed is the grim end of a cruel story. But it need not be. For in all our lives there are angels whispering promises of joy at the fringes of our consciousness. Stars appear on our bleakest horizons and beckon us to follow where we had not thought to go. Bethlehem was not on our map before: it is only when we reach the Christmas point in our journey, perhaps after a long Advent, that we know that our pilgrimage has really begun at last. The turning point of winter is an end of fear and a beginning of joy. Christmas is our first inkling that there really is more to life than we ever imagined or hoped for. And as we let go of the winter of our dreary past there is the promise for us too of spring and summer. It is the birth of this joy in our hearts that alone gives glory to God and offers peace to our world.

A famous epigram sometimes quoted in the more serious Christmas cards sums up our personal predicament: "Though Christ be born a thousand times in Bethlehem but not in you, you'll still be forever lost."

Though Christ be born a thousand times in Bethlehem but not in me....

III.

Let us go to Bethlehem and see this thing that has happened which the Lord has made known to us.

Christmas, brothers and sisters in Christ, rekindles in us memories of innocence, memories of childhood when we had every reason to believe and to hope that life would be kind to us and that we could be kind in our turn to all we would meet along the highways and by-ways of our life's journey. That is, no doubt, why we try so hard at Christmas - and risk, in fact, missing the simple truth that is there waiting for us all in the invitation to make afresh this yearly pilgrimage to Bethlehem and kneel again in adoration at the crib.

If we only but knew it, we are offered, in Christmas, the grace to become as children again. For our hope of salvation dawned on this holy night when, as we believe, God himself entered our world as a little child. Everyone who welcomes this child into their heart receives the grace to become themselves a child of God. This is the miracle of Christmas - that God chooses our hearts as a crib for his own birth, sharing in our humanity so that we can be drawn into his divinity, his God-ness, his goodness.

Christmas reveals to us afresh the healing power of a genuine reverence before all that is human in ourselves and in others, the miracle of Bethlehem that happens in our lives too when we take upon ourselves the mind and heart of those who were there that night: Mary and Joseph and the shepherds, all of them entrusted with a personal message from an angel, a message to be shared and broadcast - for the glory of God and the salvation of the world.

Mary, already filled with wonder at the conception and birth of her child, is astonished even more by what the shepherds have to tell about what they have seen and heard. Their experience confirms her own amazement. She quietly treasures the miracle of Bethlehem, taking it into her heart and she will ponder it, in joy and in sorrow, all the days of her life, and indeed for all eternity.

Venite, adoremus! Let us go to Bethlehem to adore the Saviour who has been given to us, Christ the Lord.

Midnight Mass: Isaiah 9:1-7 / Titus 2:11-14 / Luke 2:1-20

The Holy Family of Jesus, Mary and Joseph

Let the message of Christ, in all its richness, find a home with you. Teach each other, and advise each other, in all wisdom.

On this Feast of the Holy Family, brothers and sisters in Christ, the Old Testament reading reminds us each year, in the aftermath of Christmas, about the Fourth Commandment: Honour your father and your mother - and that reading from Colossians reminds us that all our relationships with one another are to be ruled by the fundamental principles of Christian morality: compassion, humility and patience in the service of love and peace.

Jesus, Mary and Joseph make a highly unusual family, it is true, and we may well wonder in what sense it is that they are recommended to us as a model for our inspiration. The first trap we fall into in life is the innocent assumption that our own family situation is entirely normal and our first surprise in life is often the discovery that other families we come to know even a little can be remarkably and radically different. Perhaps, indeed, the notion of "the normal family" is merely a theoretical construct that can never do justice to the complexities of real life.

In common with every other family, the Holy Family from the beginning were to experience their own special situations, difficulties and anxieties arising from circumstances far beyond their control. The census of Caesar Augustus obliged Mary, on the verge of giving birth, to leave home and make for Bethlehem where there was no room for them at the inn and so her child was to be born in a stable and laid in a manger. King Herod's paranoia about the possibility of a royal rival forced Joseph to flee into Egypt with mother and child and then, when it seemed safe to return to Judaea, fear of Herod's successor counselled him to settle instead in Galilee and at

Nazareth.

Throughout all this uncertainty they knew themselves in the hands of God. God's Word dwelt with them in a particularly powerful way and they lived in constant thankfulness, Mary never ceasing from her Magnificat as she treasured the Bethlehem events and pondered them in her heart.

We forget in our sentimentality that it was probably just as dark and cold and unwelcoming on that night in Bethlehem as it can be anywhere in the world on any night of the year for the wrong people in the wrong place. We forget that God's incarnation in Jesus, the Word made flesh and dwelling amongst us, means that God knows from the inside all the precariousness that we experience in our lives. The Son of God is truly made human in Jesus. Born of Mary, he grew in wisdom and age and grace in a human family. In his childhood years, Jesus did as we all do. He forged his own personal take on the human condition.

So Jesus understands what it is for so

many of the details of the individual human life to be determined by world events and local politics. He knows the fragility of human life and the dangers that lurk in every moment. This is the framework within which he submits in all things to the will of his Father for him and so accomplishes the work of our salvation that will lead him through the cross to resurrection. It is the same framework within which each of us is called in Jesus to work out our salvation in fear and trembling. We are not to look for God anywhere else, for he is nowhere if not in the circumstances of our everyday lives that we share with our families and our communities as time carries us inexorably towards death and eternity.

The invitation of today's feast is to place our renewed commitment to Christian family values at the top of our concerns for the new year, aspiring to live as Jesus, Mary and Joseph did at Nazareth, in constant thankfulness, at peace with one another and with God.

Glorifying the Lord by Your Life

Ecclesiasticus 3:2-6. 12-14 / Colossians 3:12-21 / Matthew 2:13-15. 19-23

The Holy Family

B.

The child's father and mother stood there wondering at the things that were being said about him.

Mary and Joseph, brothers and sisters in Christ, will often have wondered at the child so strangely entrusted to them by God. They will have wondered too at themselves, their lives and destinies so different from whatever they may have been expecting. Our lives too are marked by uncomfortable moments of bewilderment and uncertainty. Simeon and Anna, we might say, are more consciously and more confidently in the right place at the right time. They are close to the end of their lives and they have garnered the wisdom of long years of prayer and commitment.

On that day the Temple, so soon to be destroyed and yet for so long the symbol of God's presence with his people, welcomes Jesus the long awaited Messiah. Jesus has come to be the presence of God in the world for the rest of time. This presence of

God in the world is by no means a comfortable thing: Simeon prophesies that Jesus is destined for the fall and for the rising of many in Israel, destined to be a sign that is rejected so that the secret thoughts of many may be laid bare. Not even the mother of Jesus will be spared - a sword will pierce her soul too. And yet Simeon as an upright and devout Jew had looked forward to the comforting of Israel and he saw the child Jesus as the rising source of that comforting. There is no contradiction here, but rather a reminder that for Jesus as indeed for his disciples after him, there is no comfort outside the truth. It is because he offers us the truth that sets us free that Jesus is salvation for all, light to the nations and the glory of his race.

The truth that sets us free, the truth that is salvation, light and glory. This is something about life and about who we are that discipleship discloses to us over a lifetime. It is not something that can be fully conveyed in words from one person to another. Simeon was ready - so it was enough for him to hold the child in his arms. Anna was ready - so it was enough for her to see the child as she came by at that moment. Once we have begun to long for the coming of truth as Simeon and Anna did we can sense what we are looking forward to by considering its opposite and its absence. That at least is all too familiar. All the pain and anguish we have suffered because of the lies we have been told by people who owed us the truth. And all the dreary lies with which we decorate our lives as a false comforting in place of the truth that could set us free.

Truth emerges somewhere in the difference between Simeon and Anna and the likes of us. They are fully aware that they are in the right place at the right time. Perhaps it has not yet dawned on us, as it surely did on Mary and Joseph, that those who fear the Lord and walk in his ways are always in the right place at the right time. It is in that dawning that we, as disciples of Jesus, when we are ready, receive our salvation. We become light to others in the pagan darkness of our time and place. We give glory and praise to God our Father - and in return receive the gift of wisdom, the meaning of our lives.

Ecclesiasticus 3:2-6. 12-14 / Colossians 3:12-21 / Luke 2:22-40

C.

You are God's chosen race, his saints. He loves you, and you should be clothed in sincere compassion, in kindness and humility, gentleness and patience.

Christmas, brothers and sisters in Christ, whether we like it not, brings us face to face with the truth about our families. Mary and Joseph will often have wondered at the child so strangely entrusted to them by God. They will have wondered too at themselves, their lives and destinies so different from whatever they may have been expecting.

This feast of the Holy Family invites us to renew our sense of wonder at the people who have been so intimately entrusted to us by God in our own families. One great sadness in family life is that we get so used to one another. We lose our sense of wonder. We will not allow these people to step out of their familiar moulds and surprise us. We forget that while they have indeed been entrusted to us they never belong to us nor we to them.

A proper sense of wonder leads to respect. We stop dictating to the members of our families how they should be and we learn compassion, a compassion that extends to ourselves and the wider human family. The kindness and humility, the gentleness and patience that Colossians speaks of are the fruits of this compassion learned within the trials and vicissitudes of family life.

Such virtues are not taught by word and example. Rather they are learned through a kind of necessary suffering. Forgiveness, the highest form of compassion, is never cheaply bought. Bear with one another; for-give each other as soon as a quarrel begins. It is easier said than done as we all know. A facility for forgiveness is a grace that matures slowly through our experience of betrayal. Love and peace are the rewards of a long commitment.

Any renewal of family life that may be hoped for at this time depends on our refusal to give up on one another. It is a special grace that Christian witness offers to a society where the family as we have known it is challenged in so many ways. Such a grace begins in wonder and grows through respect into love.

Ecclesiasticus 3:2-6. 12-14 / Psalm 127 / Colossians 3:12-21 / Luke 2:41-52

Mary, the Holy Mother of God (1ˢᵗ January)

As for Mary, she treasured all these things and pondered them in her heart.

At the beginning of a new year, brothers and sisters in Christ, it is quite usual for us, more or less seriously, to make some resolutions affecting the ordinary conduct of our lives. For a Christian there is one resolution that will always be first on the list: the resolution to be more serious about prayer. To the extent that we have made our own the perspective of the non-believers who live around us and among us it will be difficult for us to attach much meaning or value to prayer. The world we live in no longer shares the astonishment at the Christmas story that was the experience of those who were there on that first Christmas night in Bethlehem long ago. The world today sees only the fragile material surface of reality and knows nothing of the deep hidden richness of the individual human personalities that embody it. Jesus came to teach us that it is the human person alone that imparts meaning and value to all the rest. Jesus became one of us to show us what we too can become in the glory of God that lights up our lives and is our destiny, our final destination.

To take this seriously is to pray. To pray like Mary who treasured her Christmas experience and pondered it in her heart. To pray like those shepherds who went back glorifying and praising God for all they had seen and heard. For us to pray is simply to take Jesus seriously, to invite him to take over the direction of our lives, to be guided by his Holy Spirit rather than the spirit of our selfish self-obsession which, if we are honest enough to admit it, is what usually decides what we actually do and what we don't do.

Prayer is not prayer unless it affects the way we live our lives. And it affects our lives by opening up for us the possibility that we are not, as we are so often tempted to think, the centre of the universe but, much

more significantly, children of God
destined to inherit his kingdom. In
prayer we learn not to see others as
rivals in a perpetual rat-race. In
prayer we learn not to see others as
enemies we need to destroy to ensure
our own survival. Prayer enables us
to see our fellow human beings as
equals to be befriended and support-
ed as an expression of God's love for
them and for us. Prayer teaches us
that it is indeed more blessed to give
than to receive.

Such is real prayer. The prayer of the
children of the one Father. The
prayer of the many brothers and
sisters of Jesus in the one family of
God. An urgent priority among the
good resolutions for the future for all
who are serious about their discipleship. It has nothing to do with
assailing the gates of heaven with
demands for things we think we
need. Almost always a better prayer
would be to ask for the grace do
without what we haven't got and
cannot have. It is Mary who shows
us what prayer is. Like her we learn
to pray when we treasure our
experience of Jesus and his gospel

and ponder it every day in our hearts. We too pray when we glorify and praise God for all that he has done for us in Jesus our Saviour. Such is real prayer, an urgent priority among our resolutions for this new year and for every new year to come until time ends and we are with God forever in his eternal glory.

May the Lord bless you and keep you. May the Lord let his face shine on you and be gracious to you. May the Lord uncover his face to you and bring you peace.

Numbers 6:22-27 / Galatians 4:4-7 / Luke 2:16-21

Second Sunday after the Nativity

The Word was made flesh, he lived among us, and we saw his glory.

This first Sunday of the new year, brothers and sisters in Christ, affords us a quiet moment to reflect again on the true meaning of Christmas, the meaning of Christmas for us. The traditional story that has been our meditation in these Christmas days is, of course, splendidly conveyed by the gospels of Matthew and Luke. With them we have followed the shepherds and knelt in wonder at the Bethlehem crib. We have joined in the angels' song. We have shared the joy of Mary and Joseph and like them we have pondered all these things in our hearts. And in celebrating Epiphany, we shall return to the crib with the wise men who came guided by their star to do homage to the child Jesus revealed to the world as the Saviour of us all.

The Prologue of St John's Gospel that we hear today approaches the

Christmas message at a different level. The Word was made flesh, he lived among us, and we saw his glory. This is the substance of Christmas that we are to take with us into the new year as we take down the cards, dismantle the crib and put away shepherds and angels and stars until they are needed again. The Word was made flesh, he lived among us, and we saw his glory.

To put this another way: A light now shines in the darkness. Like John the Baptist in his day we are sent as witnesses to speak for that light. We are not ourselves the light - something that needs to be said over and over again for it is a great temptation for those who are at all religious somehow to imagine that they themselves are the light.

Nonsense, we are not the light. We are only witnesses. But we are sent to speak for the light. And here our lives will always be more eloquent than any words we may attempt to utter. For, unlike that divine Word, our words, on their own, are never very convincing. We can, in fact, say whatever we like. What we truly believe is revealed, whether we like it or not, in how we live. The light alone is convincing. It shines through the human lives it has so gloriously transfigured.

The Word became flesh, he lived among us, and we beheld his glory. In Jesus God veils his divinity and reveals his humanity. It is in the humanity of our God made visible in Jesus that we see ourselves as we were meant to be, as we are called to be, as we can still hope to become. We miss the point of God's walking our earth in Jesus if we imagine that we can somehow get to heaven without ever having been truly on earth ourselves. For we are called to be fully human, like Jesus, and fully part of our human world. If we are to bear witness to the light we must first of all be grounded in reality and in its truth. For the glory of God that Jesus came to reveal is a human being who is fully alive in time and space, here and now, today, a light shining in the dark, a light that darkness cannot overpower.

Such is the challenge of bringing the true substance of Christmas with us into the new year, the challenge of bestirring ourselves to light our own small candle rather than forever sitting around muttering about the dark.

Ecclesiasticus 24:1-2. 8-12 / Ephesians 1:3-6. 15-18 / John 1:1-18

The Epiphany of the Lord

I.

At this sight you will grow radiant, your heart throbbing and full.

We celebrate Epiphany, brothers and sisters in Christ. The presence at the crib of the wise men from the East reminds us that the child born in Bethlehem is not the private property of Mary and Joseph. He has come from God to share our human condition and save us from our sins. He is not the saviour of his own people only but of all humanity, the saviour of every man and woman of every time and place, the saviour of every human being who has ever lived or ever shall live. Epiphany is the revelation to the world of who Jesus is, the saviour of us all.

Epiphany invites us to take our place with the wise men at the crib. That invitation makes Epiphany a very personal event. Epiphany happens for me when I am seized by the hope that Jesus might be my saviour too. Epiphany passes me by when I am content with myself the way I am. Perhaps I don't feel any need to be saved, or perhaps I am too sure that I am saved already. In fact I am a sinking ship and the first act of my saviour will be to throw my most treasured possessions overboard into the sea so that I can stay afloat. But that is not how I see it and, like Herod, my first reaction is to stop at nothing to keep such a saviour out of my space. I am armed to the teeth against salvation and no matter how often Epiphany threatens me I insist on going my own way, doing my own thing, stubbornly determined to go down gloriously with my own treasure-laden ship.

Herod was hardly a bad man as kings went. He was old and soon to die. He felt threatened. All he wanted was to hold on to what he valued, all that he had fought for over a lifetime. We need to vilify him if we are to pretend that we are different. But we are not so very different. Before Epiphany evil finds a welcome in every human heart when push comes to shove.

Jesus eludes the Herods of this world and befriends instead those who are ready to leave everything to follow their star and obey their dream. He accompanies them through the trauma of detachment as they let go of all that holds them back. He leads them gently along his own path of love and service and introduces them to a new and unsuspected happiness that changes them from the inside out. Every moment we spend in prayer is a chance for Epiphany. If it doesn't happen for us today it could just be that we are not yet ready for the journey. We mistake our poverty for riches and fear that we have too much to lose. Still, at the core of our being, we know that to miss our star and forget our dream is to lose everything.

II.

Arise, shine out, for your light has come, the glory of the Lord is rising on you, though night still covers the earth and darkness the peoples.

Epiphany, brothers and sisters in Christ, is a moment of revelation, a moment in which we realise something important about God and about ourselves. Epiphany reveals Jesus as Saviour not only of his own people but Saviour of every human being who has ever lived or ever will live. Jesus is your Saviour too, and mine. And when we are saved something happens to us. We let go of our own agenda and start to live for the salvation of others. We live no longer for ourselves alone but for him, Jesus, who died and rose again for us, sending the Holy Spirit from his Father as his first gift to all who believe in him. That is Jesus' first gift to all of us who believe in him. The Holy Spirit through whom we live no longer for ourselves but for him. The Holy Spirit, the fullness of grace in our hearts enabling us to complete the work of Jesus in our world.

Perhaps it is too painful to hear such a thing. It seems altogether remote from our everyday experience of reality. And yet that verse from the ancient prophet resonates in our hearts with an almost desperate relevance. Arise, shine out, for your light has come, the glory of the Lord is rising on you, though night still covers the earth and darkness the peoples.

Yes, such is the message of today's feast of the Lord's Epiphany for us. This is no denial of reality. Night indeed still covers our own particular bit of earth, and darkness its peoples, in so many obvious and less obvious ways. But we are called to make a difference. In Jesus our light has come, his glory overwhelms us and we in our turn become light for one another and for the world in which we live.

Epiphany measures our failure and reminds us of our hope. The Herods of this world will always manipulate religion for their own vile purposes. Go and find out all about the child, he says, and when you have found him, let me know, so that I too may go and do him homage. But in every generation there are wise men and women who follow their star and obey their dream. The Herod in our hearts tells us to make our stand where we are and defend what we have even if it means the slaughter of the innocent. Epiphany urges a different way, the way of letting go and moving on, the way of Jesus that is an end in itself, the beginning of hope, the promise of light, a new dawn for humanity.

III.

The sight of the star filled them with delight, and going into the house they saw the child with his mother Mary, and falling to their knees they did him homage.

Epiphany, brothers and sisters in Christ, is what happens when we arrive at the heart of the mystery. We know, even as we are known. Today's feast celebrates our own arrival at the crib. We are no longer strangers standing outside, staring. We have been invited in. God has appeared in our world in human form. He looks for any opportunity of grace to make his presence felt in every human life. Every moment of grace is an epiphany: every con-version, every new insight, every new stage of spiritual growth.

The crib and the gospel show us only the arrival of the wise men in Bethlehem. But there has been a journey. And there is a new road to travel, a return home by a different route. Today's feast celebrates, of course, the great truth that Jesus is the Saviour of us all, of every man and woman who has ever lived or ever will live. But that will always seem a rather extravagant claim if we our-selves, you and me, are not in some way seen to be saved, are not in some way aware that we have been saved, and do not, in some way hope to persevere to the end despite every-thing that seems to go wrong in our lives.

And so we are to look for epiphanies in our own journey and in the journeys of those whom life has entrusted to our care and guidance. Epiphany, we may be sure, respects the uniqueness of each person. We prepare for our own as best we can, and we help others prepare for theirs. And then we wait for grace to seize its own moment, for epiphany is always sheer gift.

The experience of the wise men helps us to identify a true epiphany when it happens in our own lives. Like them, we know that we have arrived, however momentarily, after a long journey, into a sacred place from which we had felt somehow excluded. The sight of the star filled them with delight, and going into the house they saw the child with his mother Mary, and falling to their knees they did him homage. They knew that this was right. With their human eyes they saw only a child and its mother. But in their hearts and souls they knew themselves admitted to the divine presence. And they returned to their own country, by a different way, to live differently, a new and fuller life.

Isaiah 60:1-6 / Ephesians 3:2-3. 5-6 / Matthew 2:1-12

The Baptism of the Lord

Because God was with him, Jesus went about doing good and curing all who had fallen into the power of the devil.

As we take a last look at the crib, brothers and sisters in Christ, and leave Christmas behind for another year, the Church invites us to jump some thirty years across the hidden life of Jesus with Mary and Joseph at Nazareth to the beginning of his public ministry marked by his Baptism by John in the river Jordan.

And if the hidden life of Jesus reminds us of the hiddenness that must be part of every human life that is not utterly trivial, the few brief months of his public ministry tell us clearly that there comes a time in the life of every man and woman when we are called upon to stand up and say who we are and what we believe in, what we strive to live for and what, if anything, we are prepared to die for. Jesus in his life has established the pattern of the lives of those who believe in him. For he is the Son of God. It is on him that the Father's favour rests.

Jesus has come to invite us to become adopted children of his Father. This is the meaning of the gift of the Holy Spirit in our own Baptism. Jesus has left us to carry on his work in the world of today. This is our understanding of the out-pouring of the Holy Spirit in the Sacrament of Confirmation. We are sent to bring the good news of forgiveness and peace to all those who have not already been touched by it, to all those who have perhaps been touched by it but not yet entirely charmed by it, and not least perhaps to one another in a per-manent renewal of our commitment to our own various discipleships.

Jesus in his life has established the pattern of the lives of those who believe in him. Sons and daughters of God our Father through the life of Jesus in us, we know that the path he has laid down for us leads to resurrection and life. We know too, and this is the condition of our realism and our sincerity, that the path Jesus asks us to follow passes through the cross and that at the heart of the cross there is the darkness of death. Jesus went about doing good and curing all who had fallen into the power of the devil. When we are truly Christian we will be seen to be carrying on this same ministry in whatever way is possible and appropriate in our own personal circumstances.

The prophet Isaiah puts it more poetically. I, the Lord, have called you to serve the cause of right. I have taken you by the hand and formed you. I have appointed you as covenant of the people and light of nations - to open the eyes of the blind, to free captives from prison, and those who live in darkness from the dungeon. And he gives us advice too on how this is to come about. He does not cry out or shout aloud, or make his voice heard in the streets. He does not break the crushed reed nor quench the wavering flame. The Gospel is not passed on in angry argument or destructive criticism but gently, in the silence of love.

John the Baptist in his day created a feeling of expectancy around him everywhere he went. Our misfortune is our forgetfulness. For we have, in fact, already been baptised and con-firmed in Jesus' name with the Holy Spirit. That Holy Spirit must surely be a source of strength and power and effectiveness. And if we have no experience of what we might call our own Christian efficiency perhaps we need to search our hearts and wonder why. For salvation is now or not at all. It is today that the world needs the healing, transforming effect of God's Holy Spirit of love.

Year A: Isaiah 42:1-4. 6-7 / Acts of the Apostles 10:34-38 / Matthew 3:13-17

Printed in Poland
by Amazon Fulfillment
Poland Sp. z o.o., Wrocław

67615430R00056